Steam Pirates

Andy Briggs ■ Dynamo

TEAM X

Max, Cat, Ant and Tiger are four ordinary children with four extraordinary watches. When activated, their watches allow them to shrink to micro-size.

MAX — hologram communicator

CAT — magni-scope, tracking device

ANT — flip-up camera, video recorder

TIGER — warning light, torch

Previously ...

The watches were running low on power. Ant tried to recharge them using a machine that he had invented. However, during this process, something in the watches changed irrevocably.

When all the watches are synchronized, the micro-friends can travel through a rip in the fabric of space and time to other dimensions. Max, Cat, Ant and Tiger have become *rip-jumpers*.

Unfortunately, there is a problem. The rip has become permanently stuck open ... in Tiger's wardrobe! This leaves Earth – our Earth – open to attack.

A woman called **Perlest** came through the rip saying she wanted to help. She told the children that they need to find the **Weaver**. Only he can seal the rip shut forever.

Now the children are trying to find Perlest's hidden thoughts – contained in **thought vials** – which will help them to track down the Weaver.

Chapter 1 – **Recollections**

Pictures fleetingly appeared amongst the swirling smoke in the thought vial, moving in a series of jerky images. They lacked definition and quickly blended into one another like a badly animated movie, or so Tiger thought.

Standing in the centre of Tiger's room, Perlest held the vial up to the light bulb and peered more closely at the memory contained within. The light seemed to add more detail to the smoky images. She removed the cork and arced her hand across the room, spilling the contents into the air.

Max, Cat, Ant and Tiger watched as the vapour billowed and formed images so rapidly that it was difficult to keep up. Was that a ship? Some kind of mechanical weapon? Now released from the vial, the images came with a torrent of sounds: the grinding sound of machinery, the hiss of steam, and multiple voices speaking rapidly and all at once. A potent smell lingered in the air – the scent of smoke and burning wood.

Then it was suddenly all over as the thought shimmered across Perlest's face and seeped into her skin. She lifted her arms to the ceiling and closed her eyes. Then her eyes flicked open again and she turned to face the friends with a smile.

'I foresee where you should go next in your search for the Weaver,' she said, in a voice so low it was almost a whisper. 'Or at least the location of the next thought vial. And you won't fail me, or make things more difficult than they should be, will you children?'

Cat harrumphed; she wasn't happy about Perlest's increasingly rude attitude towards them. 'Don't forget we are doing *you* a favour by finding him.'

Perlest's smile evaporated like water in a desert. She turned so quickly that Cat jumped. Perlest prodded a slender finger in Cat's direction.

'Don't be so insolent!' Perlest said coldly. '*You* tore the rip open, don't forget. I am helping to repair *your* mistakes!'

Cat's lips went tight. She was about to answer back, but Ant nudged her with his elbow.

Perlest didn't seem to notice. She opened Tiger's wardrobe and stared at the portal shimmering inside. The air popped and crackled around the edges and the rip looked, if possible, a little bigger than last time. It seemed to mesmerize Perlest as she stared at it.

Max was the first to break the silence. 'So, where are we going?'

Perlest blinked, as if waking from a daydream. She turned to them and smiled sweetly. 'An *elevating* place. Set your watches for dimension **8419**.'

Max peered at the portal and nodded. 'OK, everybody, follow me. Let's do this.'

Ant stepped up to the portal and grinned. 'Geronimo!' he bellowed as he leapt through. The others saw him shrink as the portal sucked him in.

'Better not keep your friend waiting,' Perlest purred. 'There will undoubtedly be dangers beyond.'

Before Tiger could answer, Cat pulled him through the rip. Max saw his friends rapidly diminish in size before vanishing. He took a step to follow them, but Perlest held him back.

'You should be careful of Tiger,' she said. 'He doesn't want you in charge.'

'Well, I'm not exactly …'

Perlest gripped his shoulder hard and looked him in the eyes. Her gaze was so intense that Max felt his eyes watering. 'But who else is better suited to lead, Max? He's jealous of you. Believe me, with everything I have been through with Vilana …' her voice broke and she looked away.

'Tiger's not like that,' Max replied. 'He's my friend. I trust him completely.'

'That's what I thought about Vilana,' Perlest said in an unsteady voice. 'And she's my sister. I had even more reason to trust her.' She pulled herself together. 'Of course, you know best, Max.'

Her smile didn't quite reach her eyes. Max couldn't think of anything reassuring to say, so he simply nodded and stepped into the portal.

He didn't look back. If he had done, he might have caught the sly smile playing on the corners of Perlest's lips.

Chapter 2 – On the run

Travelling through the rip made Max feel as if he were being stretched and squished in every direction like kneaded dough. His stomach lurched as he was spat out in the new dimension.

He landed on a cobbled floor and stumbled before quickly regaining his balance. Through the soles of his trainers he felt a throbbing vibration, as if he were standing on the deck of a ship. A strong wind blew in his face; he looked up at the sky, which was a deep azure, but before Max could get his bearings Ant yanked him by the arm.

'RUN!'

Cat and Tiger were racing ahead and Max and Ant were forced to sprint to catch up. They were on a raised wooden promenade. Glancing over the rail of the walkway, Max caught sight of several decks that sloped down below them, angled like the side of an upside-down pyramid. Beyond that – and *below* them – fluffy white clouds stretched to the horizon.

A voice bellowed, 'There they are!'

Five guards appeared on the deck below, dressed in metal armour and carrying strange mechanical devices – they looked like rods connected to cylinders – on their backs. Steam leaked from various valves and gauges on the devices. The leader was pointing up at the friends.

'*SHRINK!*' Max yelled at the others, while frantically turning the dial on his own watch. His friends reacted just in time as the guards shot a jet of super-heated steam at them. Max could feel the heat as the jet passed overhead and sizzled the paint off the wall beyond.

'Why are they trying to blast us?' panted Max, as the micro-friends scurried along an alleyway which opened on to a large square filled with people and market stalls. Buildings towered around them on three sides, while the fourth side offered an elevated view across rooftops, where the occasional spire, tower and black-smoking chimney poked up from the city that stretched into the distance. Max skidded to a halt and stared in astonishment. The others stopped too, their gazes all drawn to the view.

'This isn't a boat,' cried Ant. 'It's a city!'

'A flying city!' Cat exclaimed.

'That still doesn't explain why those guards are chasing us,' said Max, dashing to shelter under a market stall and beckoning for his friends to follow.

Tiger smiled sheepishly, bending over to catch his breath. 'That would be my fault.'

Max rolled his eyes; he wasn't surprised. 'What did you do this time?'

If Tiger detected the annoyance in Max's voice he didn't show it. 'A guard stopped me and asked to see my papers, so I just panicked and ran. Before I knew what was happening there were guards with whistles materializing everywhere.'

'That was a stupid thing to do!' said Max.

Tiger scowled. 'Well, you took your time! If you had come through the rip a bit quicker …'

'THEY MUST BE SOMEWHERE AROUND HERE!' yelled another guard, as he sprinted into the square. He was pointing wildly, causing every eye in the square to turn towards him.

The children huddled together under the stall, their faces centimetres from the guard's heavy, black boots. A movement from behind Tiger made him instinctively glance around. Towering over them was a seagull, its dead-eyed stare fixed upon them as it cocked its head to one side.

'Umm … we have company,' Tiger whispered.

Ant gasped as he turned to see the bird glaring down at them. The friends bundled out from under the stall with the seagull following close behind. The bird dipped its head down, about to peck at them. Faced with the prospect of being eaten alive, they turned the dials on their watches and returned to normal size.

The guard swung around in confusion as they appeared behind him. 'THERE THEY ARE!' he bellowed, pointing towards them with his steam rod.

Tiger turned to run, but the crowd around the friends moved as one to block their path. Tiger knew they wouldn't be fleeing anywhere. When he span round, the guards had already caught up with them, vapour drifting from the barrels of their steam rods. None of the friends dared move.

'Intruders!' spat the guard. 'You're under arrest by order of the Imperial Guard!'

The next moments were a blur as the friends were led through narrow winding streets that offered nothing more than glimpses of the sky above. They passed beneath huge golden gates on top of which perched sculptures of mighty eagles, with wings outstretched and claws poised to catch prey.

They continued around a curving iron bridge. Ant risked a glance below and saw massive pistons powering back and forth, choking smoke pumping from countless vents. He guessed it was the machinery that kept the city afloat but, before he could investigate further, a guard grabbed him by the scruff of the neck and dragged him back in line.

Once over the bridge, they entered a part of the city that was obviously the seat of power. Here the buildings were plated with curved brass, bronze and gold stretching several storeys high. The friends were nudged towards an egg-shaped building with the words *Imperial Chambers* etched in bold letters across the top.

'Looks like an important place,' muttered Cat under her breath.

'Which I think means we're in big trouble,' added Ant.

'Just let me do the talking,' said Max.

Tiger gave him a sideways glance, but didn't say anything.

A pompously-dressed guard intercepted them at the entrance.

'I am the Captain of the Guard,' he announced. 'When we enter here, you will only speak when spoken to.'

The friends were marshalled into an elegant circular chamber lit by a huge oil-burning chandelier. At the opposite end was a large, metal throne with the same eagle motif they had seen on the bridge.

'Wow!' exclaimed Ant, his voice echoing around the room.

Tiger couldn't resist putting his finger in his mouth and making a loud *POP* that bounced around the chamber. He was about to do another but stopped when he saw the disgusted look the Captain of the Guard was giving him.

'Kneel,' commanded the Captain of the Guard.

The four friends exchanged glances, but nobody was in the mood to argue. They slowly knelt before the throne and became aware of movement in the shadows. The man who appeared was squat and as wide as two of the friends. He wore a long, flowing cloak made of fine chain links that shimmered in a rainbow of colours. The man's broad nose wrinkled when he saw the four friends. He put his hands behind his back and squinted.

'*These* are the intruders?' he said dismissively.

'Yes, Your Imperial Majesty,' replied the Captain of the Guard, his eyes fixed on his toes.

'Pirates?'

'Pirates!' exclaimed Tiger, before Max could stop him. 'Do we *look* like stinking pirates?'

The squat man jerked upright in surprise; he wasn't used to being spoken to so directly. His brow scrunched in annoyance and he unclipped a baton hanging from his belt. He whirled it menacingly.

'Do you know who you are speaking to?' he demanded. 'I am His Royal Majesty, Lord Aerialas, ruler of Eagle Mount, the mightiest city empire. I am master of all you see, and *you* are nothing more than intruders and trespassers. And since the only trouble we have here is with those troublesome steam pirates …'

Aerialas squeezed the baton's handle and struck the nearest guard. The guard yelped before collapsing stunned on the floor. Lord Aerialas waved the stun-stick at the friends. 'Children or not, we have no mercy for pirates.'

'We're not pirates,' mumbled Max.

'We're just looking for something,' Tiger added.

Lord Aerialas raised a thick, caterpillar-like eyebrow. 'Oh?'

'A glass vial. About this big.' Tiger indicated with his hands. 'Looks like there's smoke inside and …' he trailed off, noticing the look on Lord Aerialas's face.

'The Eye of the Sun!' Aerialas exclaimed, staggering to his throne.

'Well, we've never heard it called that before,' said Tiger. 'But if you know where it is then we can just take it and leave you in peace.'

Lord Aerialas started quivering with rage, his cheeks flushed with anger as he stabbed a finger towards the children.

'Take it? Thieves!' Aerialas spluttered. 'You will face the same fate as every other steam pirate and walk the plank!'

DIMENSION 8419
EAGLE MOUNT

Eagle Mount was once a small flying province called Sparrow's Nest. Its ambitious mayor set out on a plan to grow the province, acquiring more and more land until it became the mega-city it is today. The flying metropolis continues to travel the dimension, in search of smaller cities to acquire.

Eagle Mount utilizes moisture in the air to create the vast amounts of steam needed to power it. Trading ships bring essential supplies, such as food, spare parts and building materials, allowing Eagle Mount to stay in flight constantly.

VITAL STATISTICS:

Number of inhabitants: 1.3 million
Number of cogs: around 784 million
Number of mechanics required to keep it in flight: 157,693

Chapter 3 – Free fall

'Well, that could've gone better,' remarked Ant, his voice trembling.

The wind blew through his hair, and he couldn't control his quivering legs as he was pushed forward to join his friends on the end of the wooden plank. Afraid of heights, he screwed his eyes closed so Cat was forced to grab his arm to prevent him from walking off the side.

'Way to go,' said Max, glaring at Tiger. 'I told you I'd do the talking.'

'Well, you didn't seem to be doing a very good job of it,' grumbled Tiger.

Max ignored him and looked at his feet. The plank wobbled even more now that Ant had joined them.

'Prepare to plummet to your doom!' bellowed Lord Aerialas from the safety of the floating city.

Ant's toes poked over the edge of the plank and he felt his knees buckle as he peered into the clouds far, far below. He had no doubts they would pass right through them and fall for who knew how long before inevitably hitting …

'I can't do this!' Ant wailed. His acrophobia was worse than facing the guards' steam rods. He was feeling dizzy and doubted his legs would carry him along the plank.

Everything happened in a swift blur. Ant caught sight of movement in the corner of his eye as something swooped from under the city – a quick glimpse of broad wings, like an enormous hunting eagle – then Lord Aerialas and the guards were shouting in alarm. The next thing Ant knew, there was a colossal *BOOM* and the entire plank shook.

That's when he fell.

He felt Cat grab his arm, but he only succeeded in pulling her over, too. As he dropped, he saw Max and Tiger clinging on to the plank for a few seconds before they slipped off as well.

The roar of the air around Ant's ears was almost deafening, but he could still make out the others' terrifying screams and the thundering roar of cannons firing.

Then he hit the ground. He hadn't expected to, as he hadn't even reached the clouds yet. It took his mind a few seconds to realize that he was on a sheet that was rapidly deflating. They had landed on an enormous airbag the size of their school sports hall, made from dirty canvas sheets stitched together.

The four friends whooped with delight, amazed they were still alive, as the airbag crumpled flat, forcing them to tumble against one another. When they finally felt the hard, wooden floor beneath them they sat up, taking stock of their surroundings.

They were in a vast wooden room with supporting timbers so old that they were badly rotting. The roof above their heads closed as two enormous doors were winched shut by rusting steel chains. Pipes ran across the ceiling, shaking and leaking steam. The thick, humid atmosphere made them feel as if they were in a sauna.

'We're on a ship!' said Ant as he looked around in wonder.

Cat nodded: it looked as though they were in the hold of an old galleon. She opened her mouth to agree when something caught her eye and she froze. The others turned. The airbag had deflated enough for them to notice the twenty or so grim-looking people surrounding them.

'Pirates,' breathed Tiger.

Of that there was little doubt. The people all had hard faces, unkempt beards, grubby clothes and were armed with cutlasses. None of them looked particularly friendly.

'Aye, that we are, laddie,' croaked a voice from the shadows.

The friends turned around to see a figure limp from the darkest corner. They could hear the *CLUMP-HISS* of a piston and Ant saw it was made by the man's dented brass peg leg as it moved in and out, helping him walk. The man's face was broad and his eyes piercing. He wore a hat with a skull and crossbones on it that made it obvious he was the captain. But the odd thing about him was his flowing beard that stretched to his stomach. It was formed of hundreds of tiny cogs, all whirling together so the metal beard was in constant motion.

'I be Captain Crankshaft,' said the captain, spitting his words from the corner of his mouth. 'And what prize have I just fished from those sky-lubbers? Take 'em up top so I can get a good look at 'em.'

The four friends were bundled up to the deck. The sky around them was grey as they drifted through a vast cloud bank, but they could make out enough to see they were on board an enormous galleon with billowing blood-red sails that propelled the craft through the air. If they needed any further confirmation they were on a pirate ship, then that came from the Jolly Roger flying from the tallest mast.

Max, Cat, Ant and Tiger stood side-by-side with their backs against the rail, while the pirates formed a line in front of them.

Tiger's eyes never left Captain Crankshaft as he paced in front of the children.

'Give me a reason you shouldn't be completin' the rest of your journey ground-ward,' demanded Crankshaft gruffly.

'You could just land and let us walk off,' Max suggested, sounding more confident than he felt.

Crankshaft whirled to face Max and pointed a metal finger in his face. Max couldn't help but notice that the captain's right hand was entirely false, made from brass rods and intricate chain-driven gears.

'My, don't we have a loud mouth here?' said Crankshaft. 'Anythin' that annoys old Aerialas is always worth checkin' out.'

'He thought we were pirates,' said Max.

Crankshaft looked at Max in surprise, then turned to the rest of his crew and burst into raucous laughter. The other pirates joined in, some laughing so hard that tears streamed down their cheeks.

'Y-you? Pirates?' gasped Crankshaft. 'Ye look nothing like pirates!'

Tiger raised himself to his full height – which was still much shorter than the captain. 'That's exactly what we told him.'

Crankshaft suddenly stopped laughing as he tried to work out if Tiger had just insulted him or not. He paced in front of the friends, sizing each of them up.

'You don't belong in the city,' he said. 'And ye certainly ain't no pirates. So where d'ye come from?'

'Some place far away,' Ant offered cautiously.

'Far away, eh?' Crankshaft parroted. 'Ye think me a fool?'

He gripped Ant's hand and pulled it towards the grinding cogs in his beard. Ant tried to resist and keep his fingers bunched in a tight fist, but the captain was far too strong. With his other hand he plucked a finger-sized splinter of wood from the railing behind Ant and fed it into the gnashing cogs. It crunched and splintered as the metal beard pulped the wood.

'No!' gasped Ant. 'I'm telling the truth!'

Crankshaft forcibly extended Ant's index finger and edged it towards the grinding mechanism.

'Don't sound truth-like to me,' growled the captain.

Ant tightly closed his eyes. He could already sense the tiny breeze whipped up by the beard. He clenched his teeth, preparing for the pain.

'STOP!' yelled Tiger. 'He's telling the truth! We don't belong here! We're searching for the Eye of the Sun so we can get home.'

Max nudged Tiger in the ribs. 'Shut up!' he hissed. 'You and your mouth are getting us into trouble again.'

Crankshaft's eyes narrowed, and he dropped Ant's hand. 'The Eye of the Sun?' he murmured. 'That's a cursed jewel.'

The captain fell silent for a moment then muttered to a thin man wearing a rusting eyepatch who must have been his first mate. Then the captain turned to the friends and regarded them thoughtfully.

'We know Aerialas has it,' said Tiger.

'Aye,' Crankshaft nodded. 'It's at the heart of a devastatin' weapon. And that's somethin' we don't want him to have.'

'So will you help us get it?' asked Cat.

The captain treated them to a toothless smile. 'The enemy of an enemy – is a steam pirate's friend!'

Chapter 4 – **Steam pirates**

Captain Crankshaft's galleon was called the Condor, or so he told them as he walked them round the ship. He also told the friends how the ship, with its thirty-strong crew, was one of only four pirate vessels remaining in the sky since Aerialas had outlawed them, forbidden to return to the city on pain of death.

'Well, you *are* pirates,' said Ant, as if that explained everything.

Captain Crankshaft stopped his tour of the ship and glared at Ant. 'And what's that supposed t'mean?'

Ant spluttered, unable to answer. His gaze fell to Crankshaft's beard that seemed to be whirling with anger. Then he noticed that Crankshaft was laughing at him.

'That we are, laddie,' roared Crankshaft. 'But we never used t'be.' He ran his hands along a line of iron cannons: there were ten of them on either side of the galleon, all in varying states of disrepair. His shoulders sagged and his expression softened.

'I used to be mayor of a city m'self,' he sighed.

'You were a mayor?' blurted out Cat, astonished.

'Aye. Voted in by m'citizens, too. Back then the cities were much smaller, before Aerialas came along and joined 'em together in that single mega-city. He's the real pirate, I tell ye.'

Max frowned and glanced at his friends. This wasn't the shameful pirate story he had been expecting. 'Tell us what happened.'

Crankshaft took a deep breath and sat on a cannon as he gazed out into the misty sky.

'It was a good life, soarin' the skies. My people were content until we heard rumblin's of trouble on the wind. Distant cities that were not as happy as we were. On some, folks were even going hungry. Of course, we sent boats laden with food parcels and took back any who needed nursin'.' He paused for a moment and tapped the cannon with a metal finger before continuing. 'Our kindness was our mistake, ye see. We brought them in and nursed them to health, without knowin' they was mutineers ready to attack us from the inside.'

The four friends listened in silence. Max looked around and saw that the crew had all gathered around to listen, their faces masks of sadness.

Captain Crankshaft continued in a low voice. 'It was durin' a storm they came. Aerialas's ships, thronging with ruthless cut-throats armed to the teeth, attacked us. I still remember Aerialas's cruel smile as he made innocent folks walk the plank.'

Max shuddered at the thought. The captain's head sagged and the cogs on his whirling metal beard stopped turning.

'That was the last time I saw m'family,' he whispered.

'What hap–' Ant began innocently, but he stopped when he felt Cat standing on his foot. She shook her head.

Crankshaft looked thoughtfully at his crew, then went on. 'We all lost folks that night. I lost m'family … and m'leg.' He tapped the metal peg leg. Gears and chains whirled in response. 'Aerialas declared himself Sky Lord 'n' seized Eagle Mount. Anybody refusin' to live under his rule was forced over the edge. He took their freedom like that.' He clicked his metal fingers, creating a bright blue spark that quickly faded away.

The captain stood up, his fake leg loudly thumping against the deck. 'He made me walk the plank, too. But I was saved by these 'ere louts.' He nodded to his crew. 'They had the sense to take this boat and escape. They caught me, just like we plucked you outta the air.'

'We never had the chance to say thank you for that,' said Cat.

Crankshaft nodded. 'You can thank me by takin' that cursed jewel from Aerialas's possession and puttin' it far from here.'

'I don't understand what he uses the Eye of the Sun for,' said Max.

'It's the standard of the jewel, y'see,' said the captain. 'The glass is top quality, and that smoke stuff inside, it seems to magnify the light that passes through. Aerialas forced a bunch of brain-box scientists to use it to make a ferocious weapon capable of blowin' the Condor outta the sky.'

'Like a laser,' said Ant suddenly.

The captain looked confused and shrugged, evidently not knowing what a laser was. 'If y'say so, laddie. In seconds it can vaporize an entire ship. In hours it will fry any city that refuses to surrender to Aerialas's control.'

Now Crankshaft was getting angry. 'I've seen entire cities burn 'n' fall from the sky. Seen fellow rebels,' he glanced at Tiger, 'or *pirates* if you prefer, annihilated in a single flash.'

'That's awful,' murmured Cat, covering her mouth as she imagined the horrors.

'Aye, that it is, lass. We just can't get close enough to stop Aerialas.'

Silence descended across the deck, broken only by the rustle of wind in the sails and creak of the wooden deck around them. Max was thinking hard. Then he had an idea.

'What if we could get on board and take the jewel?'

'Don't ye think we tried?' the captain snapped back. 'Gettin' into the city is near impossible, and then there are the guards … and we don't even know where the weapon's control room is. Even if we did, I hear there's only one door in and out which is sealed at all times. It's impossible!'

Max smiled and looked Crankshaft squarely in the eye. 'You're forgetting, Captain, we already managed to get aboard once. And we can do it again.'

Chapter 5 – The betrayal

'I don't trust him,' said Tiger, for the third time.

'We don't have much choice,' Max pointed out, as he tried once again to climb into the hammock that was strung across the cabin they had been allocated.

'He's a *pirate*! He even calls himself a pirate! He's proud of that!' urged Tiger. 'How do we know he was telling the truth back there?'

Max grunted as he dropped into the hammock. He was rolled around as the canvas whirled beneath him – and landed on the floor.

'Could you stop arguing?' said Cat. 'We're close to getting the thought vial and finding the Weaver, so we all need to stop bickering and focus.'

Tiger looked thoughtful and said nothing. Max gave up with the hammock. He sighed then clapped his hands together and motioned for his friends to gather around. 'OK, let's go through the plan one more time.'

'*Your* plan,' muttered Tiger.

* * * * * *

Despite a bright, full moon, Tiger had never seen so many stars. It was as if paint flecks had been cast across the velvet sky. He stood at the Condor's prow and craned his neck into the night, listening to the creaking of wood and metal as the vessel cut through the sky. With nothing more than the rustling of the sails and the rhythmic hiss of wind past his ears, he felt at peace.

As soon as the sun had set, the pirate ship had left the safety of the clouds and gained altitude, altering its course back towards the city.

Tiger glanced around the deck to check he was alone, then extended a spyglass he had borrowed from the silent first mate. He scanned the sky until he spotted a bright cluster of distant lights that looked like a nebula; but they were not stars, they were the lights of Eagle Mount hanging ahead and slightly above the pirate ship's current course.

Tiger licked his lips nervously. If he was going to do this then he needed to act quickly before he chickened out. He ran to a battered lifeboat hanging over the side of the galleon. Like the Condor, the smaller boat had

two canvas wings that were currently flattened against its hull. The propeller at the back was powered by clockwork. The rest of the boat had a roof and a conical nose to allow it to slice through the air.

Tiger took a deep breath to summon his courage. He had one last look around, then climbed over the railing and slipped into the lifeboat. Once aboard he took a firm grip on a rope. One end was tied to a cleat, the other connected in an elaborate fashion to the propeller, the folded wings and the mechanism that attached the lifeboat to the Condor.

Tiger gave the rope a good tug, releasing it from the cleat. It shot through his fingers and he felt the lifeboat lurch as it plummeted downwards. As soon as the lifeboat was away from the galleon, the spring-loaded side-wings popped out to stop it falling and it soared forwards and upwards. The last length of rope attaching the lifeboat to the Condor zipped through the propeller's clockwork motor, activating a flurry of whirling cogs and gears. The lifeboat immediately surged forwards as it gained speed.

Tiger whooped with delight as he gripped the boat's controls. He spun the lifeboat in a barrel roll and cheered as he went upside-down. With the blood rushing to his head, he righted the boat and set course for Eagle Mount.

* * * * * *

Lord Aerialas disliked being woken up early. The Captain of the Guard had rung the speaking-tube constantly until Aerialas had finally picked up. His steam car had driven him at high-speed through the city to meet the Captain of the Guard at the dock.

The Captain of the Guard greeted Aerialas with a bow and led him to a small knot of guards who parted to reveal Tiger, nervously clutching a white piece of cloth to indicate his surrender.

Aerialas looked Tiger up and down, regarding him like a rat. 'Look what the wind blew in. Give me one good reason why I shouldn't throw you off the edge again?'

Tiger swallowed hard; his throat was dry. 'I came to talk. To, um, I think the word is: *parley*.'

Aerialas's eyebrow shot up questioningly. 'What could you and I possibly have to discuss?'

'Captain Crankshaft.' Tiger gave a small smile when he saw Aerialas stiffen. 'For some reason, my friends trust a certain pirate a lot more than they do me. Especially when he's planning to attack you.'

A cold smirk crept across Aerialas's face. 'Perhaps we *should* talk. After all, they don't sound like true friends to me.'

Chapter 6 – **Plan in action**

'Ahead, full speed!' roared Captain Crankshaft as he spun the ship's wheel.

Max, Cat and Ant stood on the bridge with him, shivering; the wind grew increasingly chilly as the Condor accelerated. They skimmed the clouds in the moonlight, occasionally kicking up spiralling wisps of vapour.

'I hope this plan of yours works,' said Crankshaft, with more than a trace of worry in his voice. 'It sounds too good to be true.'

'We don't have much choice now,' replied Max, clenching his jaw. He was used to being in charge. It was a heavy burden sometimes, but now that Tiger had taken matters into his own hands, Max felt powerless.

Before Tiger had left, Crankshaft had sent an urgent communiqué out to the other pirate ships, requesting that they all rendezvous as soon as possible. He'd used mechanical messenger-pigeons, nicknamed 'dodgers' due to their ability to rapidly change direction to avoid being caught.

Cat loved the dodgers, which were metal spheres, a bit bigger than tennis balls. Messages could be hidden inside or encoded on three revolving numbered dials and all pirate vessels used them as a rapid form of communication. Crankshaft had talked the friends through some other functions of the dodgers, such as the smoke bomb function, and had given them a couple in case they proved to be useful.

'Where are we heading, Captain?' asked Ant.

'Cutlass Peak. It's the last place we've got left that Aerialas ain't captured.'

'Cutlass Peak?' said Cat, tilting back a pirate's hat she had found that was a little too big. 'That sounds ominous.'

'It is,' smirked Crankshaft, 'if ye ain't a pirate. Lucky I made you all honorary ones. There!' He pointed ahead.

The sea of clouds stretched to the horizon, resembling dazzling snow under the light of the full moon. In the distance, a jagged mountain poked through the cloud, snow clinging to its flanks. The peak was curved, with two sharp pinnacles.

'Wow!' exclaimed Ant. Then he squinted. 'Are those buildings?'

Sure enough, a shanty town had been built on the sharply sloped mountainside. The wooden buildings were stacked almost on top of one another, linked by wooden walkways that spanned the dizzying heights. Steam curled from many chimneys and, even at this late hour, lights burned from within.

'There's another ship.' Cat pointed. 'Hang on, there's three of them ...'

Each of the ships looked similar to theirs, though the Condor was the only one sporting crimson sails.

'Aye,' said Crankshaft. 'We're the last to arrive, and I wager the captains'll all be eager to listen to what we have to say.'

* * * * * *

The three friends had never been in a saloon before, and entering the Wolf Skin Inn was an assault on their senses. The atmosphere was thick with steam, as hot and sickly as a swamp, and the smell ...

'Smells like a sweaty-sock factory,' said Cat in a low voice.

'You're being polite,' Ant whispered back, holding his nose. 'It smells *far* worse.'

It was packed to the roof with pirates. The noise was suddenly quelled as a hundred pairs of unfriendly eyes turned to the friends. Max flinched as somebody spat close to him. It landed with a *DING* in a spittoon next to his foot.

Three captains stepped through the throng. One was rotund with skeletal mechanical arms that hissed and wheezed every time he moved them. The second was a bald woman with metallic skin that glinted in the flickering candlelight. And the last was a small, ferrety man who, to Max, seemed the utter opposite of how a pirate should look.

The four captains stared at one another for several long moments before breaking into laughter, back slapping each other and issuing lots of *arrh*s. Eventually the captains gathered around Max, Cat and Ant and examined them critically.

'So these are your secret weapons?' sneered the woman, who had been introduced as Madison Skull.

'Don't be fooled by the way they look,' said Crankshaft, in all seriousness.

'Hey!' Ant protested, but he was ignored.

'Aerialas threw them overboard after they sneaked right into the city. I reckon they have skills enough.'

'The moment we get close to Eagle Mount, Aerialas will shoot us down,' said the huge man. 'I'm surprised you're still alive after you saved them, Crankshaft.'

Crankshaft winked. 'I'm as quick as a sparrow, y'know me.' He laid his heavy hands on Max's shoulder. 'And I believe they've got what it takes for us to win this battle once and for all.'

The ferrety captain bent over and peered at the three friends. 'And what d'you want in return for helping us? A few lollipops?'

While Cat was afraid, surrounded by the menacing pirates, she knew they wouldn't be respected if they let such an insult go unchallenged.

'Forget lollipops!' she snorted, tilting back her pirate hat. 'You could do with a sackful of mints to freshen that breath of yours.' She wafted her hand in front of her nose to indicate a bad smell.

The ferrety captain stood upright in indignation. His cheeks flushed and he tried to splutter a retort. 'Why you … I never … spoken to like … I can't …'

Crankshaft burst into laughter. 'See? They got more guts than many of you, cowerin' here and hopin' Aerialas will just fly away an' leave ye alone.' He turned serious as he faced the other pirates. 'Make your minds up *after* ye hear their plan. I assure you, not a man nor woman amongst ye will doubt their courage.'

The assembled pirates murmured to each other and, as far as Max could tell, they were agreeing to listen.

'Although,' said Crankshaft, raising a warning finger, 'ye may find the idea a little … far-fetched.'

Chapter 7 – **The deal**

At first the pirates had listened in stunned silence as Max, Cat and Ant outlined their plan and told them that Tiger had jumped ship. Then every voice in the room was talking at once.

'It's unthinkable!' a pirate snarled scornfully.

'It's genius!' called another.

Everybody else had viewpoints somewhere in between. Questions were asked and strategies examined, but the captains eventually agreed that the plan could work. It was dangerous. But it could work.

Max had insisted that they must launch the attack while it was still dark. Luckily they still had many hours before sunrise. Better still, the cloud cover was thick.

As the ships were prepared, the three friends found time to talk to the other captains. The huge captain was called Morris and, when he wasn't looking mean, he was always telling very unfunny jokes.

Ant couldn't stop staring at Captain Skull's metallic skin. He didn't stop until she whirled around and glared at him.

'What are you looking at?' she demanded.

'I, um, I was just wondering … what had happened to you?'

'Aerialas tried to boil me in molten bronze,' she muttered. 'He just didn't do a very good job.'

Ant looked at his feet and thought it best not to ask any further questions.

Nobody wanted to speak with Captain Ferret as his body odour really was bad. Even his own crew didn't want to be with him. Max had learned that he used to be a chef in one of the cities that Aerialas had captured. The thought of the state of his kitchen made Max feel queasy.

Crankshaft gave the three friends a long list of preparations to be made, and they pushed any worries about Tiger to the back of their minds.

Within the hour, the pirate galleons sailed from Cutlass Peak, led by Crankshaft and the Condor. They made terrific progress and Crankshaft observed that the winds were in their favour. Although he seemed relaxed, his beard was anxiously whirling and grinding.

After almost an hour's sailing, Max felt his eyelids drooping. It felt like an age since he had last slept.

His eyes suddenly flicked open when the Condor rocked as it hit turbulence. Had he fallen asleep for long? For a second he thought he'd imagined the shaking, but the crew were all running to their posts. Cat hurried up to him.

'What's happening?' he asked.

'Bad weather,' she replied. 'Captain said we better hold on tight!' She offered him the rope she clutched in one hand; the other end was tied to the rail.

'What kind of bad weather?' asked Max, as he looked ahead. His jaw dropped open when he saw blood-red storm clouds, moving chaotically towards them. A warning bell rang across the ship.

Crankshaft yelled at the top of his lungs. 'Rust storm ahoy!'

Within seconds, the fleet was in the thick of the storm. Crankshaft had fastened himself to the helm with a rope and gritted his teeth as the wheel bucked in his hands, the galleon shuddering from sudden violent winds.

The blasting wind made Max's eyes water and he looked away as lightning crackled through the sky, hitting the mast and shooting harmlessly from the bottom of the boat.

'We're not grounded,' Ant shouted over the storm, 'so the lightning can't do us any harm!'

Crankshaft twisted the wheel so suddenly the boat tilted and Max and Cat skidded across the deck, clutching the rope for their lives. They slammed into the railing, only to find that Ant – who had tightly secured himself there – was watching the storm with an awed expression.

'That must be a rust-whirligig!' he exclaimed. 'Crankshaft warned us about them!' He pointed to a dense red cloud that was blossoming like a flower.

'Hard to starboard!' yelled Crankshaft as the boat turned away, but the rust-whirligig stretched after them, as if seeking out the metal hull. The galleon shuddered as the cloud lashed the side, leaving a long, brown rust stain and tearing holes in the wing.

'That was close!' Ant gasped. 'I bet it would have ripped clean through the hull if we'd hit it dead on!'

The ship abruptly lurched in the other direction, and Cat and Max slid back across the deck to hit the railings on the opposite side. The Condor shot out of the clouds, rapidly leaving the storm behind.

'*HA-HA!*' yelled Crankshaft triumphantly. 'No storm's gonna swat Crankshaft outta the sky!'

Max picked himself up, feeling a little seasick – or should that be air-sick? With shaking legs, he stood and glanced behind the Condor, but couldn't see any of the other ships.

'Oh no,' said Max in despair. He ran to the helm to give Crankshaft the news.

The Captain didn't even bother turning around. 'Don't worry, lad, they're seasoned captains one and all. We ain't seen the last of them.'

Max looked back at the storm clouds. They continued to roll, as if pursuing the pirates. He hoped the other crews had escaped unharmed.

The moon lit their way as they continued towards Eagle Mount. Max stood with Crankshaft and peered at the stars. His mind strayed to Tiger. His fingers clenched around the rail of the ship.

* * * * * *

Tiger burped loudly as he finished the opulent meal. He picked the remaining bits of meat from a drumstick that was bigger than his forearm. Lord Aerialas sat down the long side of the table and peered at him from above steepled fingers.

'That was amazing chicken,' said Tiger, patting his stomach.

Aerialas looked puzzled. 'Chicken? Never heard of it. You have just eaten albatross.'

Tiger froze with the last piece of meat in his mouth. Still, it tasted good, so he swallowed and burped again in what he thought was a suitably grateful manner.

'So … they plan to attack,' Aerialas reminded Tiger.

Tiger sighed. 'Like I said, old Cog-beard has got it in for you, and he's coming tonight. Before dawn, when it's darkest.'

'With your friends,' said Lord Aerialas, still not quite sure what to make of Tiger's story.

Tiger hammered his fist against the table. 'They're not my friends. They'd rather listen to a pirate than to me!' He shook with anger. 'I'm fed up with Max always thinking he's right. Always assuming that *he's* the boss. Well, now I'm doing something about it! He'll see!'

The door opened and the Captain of the Guard rushed in, whispered something in his lord's ear, and left with equal haste. Aerialas stood, his head tilted backwards so he stared straight down his nose at Tiger.

'It appears you are correct. That fool, Crankshaft, has been spotted heading our way. The question is, what do your friends really mean to you?'

Tiger stood up and threw his napkin on the table. 'I'm ready to fight them.'

Lord Aerialas gave a thin smile. 'Splendid. You know, Tiger, you remind me of somebody. Me.'

* * * * * *

'Eagle Mount dead ahead, sir!' cried the lookout from the top of the crow's nest.

'Ready the cannons!' Captain Crankshaft bellowed in reply. 'Port side first when they come a-callin', then I'll wheel us around and unleash iron!'

'Do you think we've been spotted yet?' asked Cat anxiously, passing her dodger from palm to palm. She hoped a black ship at night would appear almost invisible, but Crankshaft soon shattered that idea.

'Undoubtedly. They have all manner of gizmos to spot us comin'. Even in the dead of night.' Despite the tension, Crankshaft grinned. 'Although if we'd stayed in that storm behind us, they wouldn't have seen a thing.'

'Incomin'!' yelled the lookout.

Cat squinted into the darkness but couldn't see anything. 'What is it?'

'Interceptors,' said Crankshaft grimly. 'Small, fast and heavily armed boats.'

'Can you outrun them?' asked Max.

'On a good day ... no,' Crankshaft replied. 'And this is a grim day. You ready, laddie?' He cocked his head toward Ant who was tinkering with his watch.

'Almost,' said Ant.

Max and Cat joined him, readying their own watches.

'Are you sure about this?' Cat asked nervously.

'Yeah. Pretty much,' said Ant.

'Pretty much?' repeated Cat in alarm. 'If you're wrong, Ant ...'

'If I'm wrong then we're going to jump and plummet to our deaths,' finished Ant. 'So fingers crossed I'm right.'

'The storm's gainin' on us!' shouted Crankshaft. 'You better do whatever it is you're doin' so we can get outta here!'

The three friends moved out of Crankshaft's line of sight. The old pirate had promised he wouldn't pry into the secret part of their plan.

'Ready?' asked Max. The others nodded. 'Then let's go!'

Cat dropped her dodger and at the same time they all turned the dials on their watches ...

Chapter 8 – The flight

It was perfect timing. As Cat dropped the dodger, wings sprung from the mechanical device's circumference and began to whirl at high speed – saving it from hitting the deck.

At the same moment, Max, Cat and Ant all jumped and shrank. The combination of falling and shrinking meant the descent seemed to last forever.

They all landed on the dodger's smooth metal surface just as the device was rising from the deck. Ant had insisted they practise below deck, landing on the dodger as it lay motionless on the floor. It had taken a lot of choreography, but after fifteen minutes of practice they had finally cracked how to jump, shrink and land without falling off.

Doing it for real, with the wind blasting on the deck and the dodger now fully activated, was a completely different matter. Max and Ant landed on the curved brass surface and immediately found handholds on the rivets that held the device together.

But Cat landed awkwardly and found herself sliding down the smooth surface. This had happened several times in training, but now the dodger's rotors whirled around the circumference at such high speed they were a blur. Cat was under no illusions that if she fell into them, she would be sliced and diced.

Ant's hand suddenly shot out and grabbed her arm, halting her descent, and pulled her to safety. Cat gripped on to a rivet, her heart beating furiously and the blasting wind sweeping away the sound of her grateful words of thanks.

The three friends clung on to the dodger as it raced towards the coordinates they had set – Eagle Mount.

Chapter 9 – The raid

THUD! Max felt his teeth jar as the dodger landed hard on Eagle Mount's top deck and began to roll so fast that the three friends were hurled off. They grew back to normal size and slid to a halt, out of breath but unscathed.

Ant flattened his hair that had been whipped up by the wind. 'I *never* want to do that again!'

Cat retrieved the dodger and slipped it back into her pocket as they took stock of their surroundings. They crept down the narrow street until they came to a railing that overlooked the decks of the city that stretched out below them.

'Now all we have to do is find the weapon control room, break in and snatch the vial,' said Max, as if it would be the easiest thing in the world.

'Let's hope they hurry up and show us where they're hiding the weapon then,' said Cat, as distant explosions flashed in the air, indicating the Interceptors had finally caught up with the Condor.

* * * * * *

Tiger was excited to be taken to the subway system used by the city's ruling elite. Lord Aerialas led him several storeys down to a massive, elegant hall the size of a major train station and panelled in polished bronze. At the centre was an enormous steel turntable on which sat a car that resembled a fighter jet. Positioned around the turntable were a dozen tunnels leading to various distant parts of the city.

'Climb aboard,' Aerialas commanded.

Tiger clambered into the rear seat. Aerialas sat in front and tugged on a lever to pull the glass canopy shut with a hiss. He industriously turned a wheel, swinging the entire car to face one particular tunnel.

'Hold tight,' he warned as he hauled back two other levers.

WHUMP! The car shot forward at such an incredible speed that Tiger was shoved back in his chair so hard the air was sucked from his chest. Before he could get his breath back, the car stopped so suddenly that he was thrown against the padded seat in front of him. Only then did he notice that he had been sitting on his seatbelt.

'Here we are,' announced Aerialas, as the canopy opened. They climbed from the car and stood on the platform of a smaller station.

'And where is *here*?' asked Tiger curiously.

'The control room for the greatest weapon the universe has ever seen.'

Aerialas led him up a spiral staircase and they entered a cavernous room filled with flickering black and white monitors and hundreds of levers, dials and cranking wheels. To Tiger's eyes it looked like the oldest technology he had ever seen, but he reasoned it was probably the most advanced in *this* dimension.

Two white-suited technicians sat at the controls, their eyes glued to the screens. Tiger could just make out a fast-moving blurry image on the screen.

'What's that?' he asked.

Lord Aerialas smiled. 'That is Crankshaft's ship, the one with your friends on board. The Interceptors are luring it closer and once it is in range, we'll blow it from the sky.' He turned to the technicians, his voice dropping to a cold command. 'Seal the chamber.'

Tiger jumped as the doorway behind him spiralled closed. Aerialas noticed Tiger's puzzled expression. 'Better safe than sorry. There is no way for any pirates to get in here now.'

'As long as we don't suffocate,' said Tiger with a nervous laugh. Aerialas gave him a questioning look.

'I don't like enclosed spaces,' Tiger explained.

Lord Aerialas pointed to a small air vent. 'Fresh air comes in there.' He turned back to the technicians. 'Energize the Eye of the Sun!'

A loud hiss and rumble shook the room. Tiger looked up as he traced the source of the noise. That's when he noticed a giant structure supporting a huge cannon, the length of a jumbo jet. At the base of the super-weapon was a cage, like a three-dimensional spider's web, in the middle of which hung a familiar glass thought vial.

A spotlight positioned under the vial gradually illuminated, becoming so bright that Tiger was forced to look away. The vial absorbed the light and the whole weapon began to shake, the rumbling rising in volume. A laser pulsed down the length of the barrel from the tip of the vial, the shape of the tiny bottle magnifying the beam's strength. It gained intensity with every passing second.

'It will take several minutes to power up,' said one of the technicians.

'Track the pirates and prepare to vaporize them,' Aerialas commanded as he clasped his hands together, watching Crankshaft's ship on screen slowly getting closer.

Tiger was sweating heavily. He moved to the air vent and took a deep breath. Things were getting very serious and he was beginning to regret being locked in this room with such a cold and ruthless man.

* * * * * *

Max, Cat and Ant had worked their way up to the highest walkway they could find in order to get a clear view across the city. Cat kept an eye on the relentless flashes out in the deep black skies, like watching a distant firework display.

'They're still attacking the Condor,' she said solemnly.

'I hope Crankshaft's going to be OK,' said Max. He had become quite fond of the old pirate.

'He knows what he's doing,' said Ant confidently. He kept his gaze across the city. Then he saw movement and pointed. 'There!'

The others followed his finger to a tower far across the city. The entire building was swathed in a veil of steam as pistons peeled the building's two halves apart like a banana skin, revealing the super-weapon beneath.

'Send the dodger back,' said Max determinedly. 'Let Crankshaft know we've found it.'

Cat pulled the sphere from her pocket. She rotated the numbered dials to indicate the code she wanted to pass on to Crankshaft, then tightened the clockwork mechanism inside. The brass device shot from her hand, heading towards the Condor.

Without another word, the three friends ran along the city's rooftop walkways towards the giant cannon as it slowly moved into position. They kept to the shadows, ducking low and hoping the guards wouldn't spot them.

* * * * * *

'We're tracking the Condor now, sir,' said one of the technicians in a flat emotionless voice. If he was concerned about destroying an entire ship and its crew, then he wasn't giving anything away.

'Good,' purred Aerialas. 'Let's draw them in.' He glanced at Tiger, who was hyperventilating as he leaned against the air vent. 'What's the matter boy?'

'Told you,' gasped Tiger. 'I hate confined spaces. Makes it difficult for me to breathe.'

Lord Aerialas sneered and turned back to the screen. Tiger had served his purpose. As soon as he had eliminated Crankshaft, the boy would be thrown overboard. For the second time.

* * * * * *

The galleon shook as an Interceptor cannon strafed the stern. Crankshaft put all his weight into turning the wheel and the Condor banked sharply starboard.

'They're comin' around again!' bellowed the lookout, whose ear stung from a close encounter with a cannon blast.

Crankshaft gritted his teeth; it was only a matter of time before the Interceptors got a lucky shot that would cripple his vessel. He ducked as something buzzed past his ear. What he had thought was another cannonball was in fact the dodger he had given to Cat. He plucked it from the air and examined the dial code on the side. It read 321 – a basic signal for the pirates to go to the next phase of the plan. He smiled grimly. Now was the time to stop running and start attacking. It also meant that very soon they could be blown out of the sky as they came within range of the devastating weapon.

'Alert the others!' he roared as he swung the galleon around on a direct course towards the city. 'We're goin' in!'

* * * * * *

Max scrambled behind a mound of smelly rubbish sacks as soon as he heard the footsteps. He pulled Ant and Cat with him, putting his finger to his lips. The footsteps grew louder ... heading in their direction. Had they been spotted?

Max heard the gentle *CLINK* of metal armour. It was a city guard patrol – and they were walking straight towards them.

Max pressed his head lower. He was pretty sure they

couldn't be seen in the shadows, but he wasn't certain.

The guards approached.

They all held their breath as the guards rounded the corner ... and walked straight past. Max gave it several seconds for the footsteps to recede before he rose from cover.

'They've gone,' he whispered.

Ant scrunched up his nose. 'The smell of that rubbish pile reminds me of Captain Ferret.'

They had covered a great distance without running into any patrols, which Max guessed meant that Lord Aerialas was arrogant enough to think nobody could have made it aboard the city. It gave him hope that their plan wasn't as desperate as Crankshaft had first supposed.

The street ended at a large city park, one of the few green spaces in the city. It would have usually been dominated by a single building, but now that building had split in half as the super-weapon had appeared from below. Steam rose from the weapon's flanks as it powered up.

'Now we have to get inside,' said Ant.

'That should be easy enough,' replied Max, pointing to a small air vent that was spewing bright green smoke. 'All we have to do is shrink to the occasion!'

Chapter 10 – **Into the den**

Lord Aerialas frowned. Something was wrong. He leaned closer in towards the screen. The Condor had changed direction and, instead of fleeing, it was now heading directly towards them.

He had expected that. That was his plan.

What he hadn't expected was for three *other* pirate ships to suddenly emerge from the nearby storm clouds.

'We couldn't detect them in the rust storm,' yelled a technician. 'They're opening fire!'

The entire city shook as the four pirate ships unleashed their cannons in unison – all targeting the exact same spot.

'They're aiming for the engines!' exclaimed the other technician in shock.

Lord Aerialas hammered his fist on the control panel. 'FIRE!'

'We can't!' exclaimed the first technician. 'They're now too close and moving too fast! We can't get a lock on them!'

Aerialas was lost for words. Too close to use his ultimate weapon? It was almost as if he had stepped into a trap …

He slowly turned to face Tiger, who had now recovered enough to have moved away from the air vent and was watching the screens.

'You must think you're clever, setting this up,' said Aerialas in a low, threatening voice. 'But all you have done is lure your friends to their inevitable doom.' He drew his stun-stick and took a menacing step towards Tiger, who retreated with his hands raised to fend the man off. 'They'll never reach me here,' growled Aerialas. 'Not through all my defences.'

Tiger shrugged. 'I'm not so sure about that.' The look of confusion that crossed Aerialas's face was almost worth the fear Tiger felt.

BAM! The air vent blew from the wall and struck Aerialas a glancing blow. He collapsed in a heap as micro-sized Max, Cat and Ant jumped from the small air duct. They grew back to normal size and the two technicians watched in astonishment as the new arrivals seemed to appear from nowhere.

Max grinned at Tiger and threw him the dodger that he had found in the air vent, still spewing green smoke. 'Here's your smoke bomb back as a souvenir.'

Tiger caught it in mid-air. 'Told you *my* part of the plan was brilliant!'

Max smiled. 'Pretending to be a traitor was a *stupid* plan,' Max corrected. 'But secretly brilliant.'

'Great to see you, Tiger,' said Cat, who had doubted the plan would work at all.

Ant nodded. 'Yup, ditto, but we'd better get on with shutting the weapon down.'

Max turned to the stunned technicians. 'Turn that thing off now!'

'W-we can't,' spluttered a suddenly talkative technician. 'Once activated, it *has to* unleash the stored energy.'

Max looked up to the sky and spotted the brightly glowing thought vial, hanging teasingly just beyond reach. 'We have to get it out somehow,' he said.

'I'm out of ideas,' replied Ant.

'The weapon is over-charging!' warned the technician, as he desperately glanced at a bank of dials. All the needles were flickering furiously in the red zones. 'It's going to explode!'

Tiger kneeled next to Aerialas and took the stun-stick from his hand. Aerialas groaned as he started to come around, but he was too groggy to stop Tiger from taking it and clambering up the structure of the weapon towards the cage housing the vial. As he climbed on to a small ledge beside the cage, Tiger could feel the intense heat emanating from the weapon and had to look away.

He could see the others shouting at him from below, but he couldn't hear them over the rumbling machine. He examined the stun-stick and noticed it had a power setting. There was only one thing for it. He slid the power to maximum, raised the stick to the metal cage around the vial and squeezed the handle as hard as he could.

Chapter 11 – Crankshaft's return

BAM! There was a bright explosion, and one of the clamps holding the thought vial broke away. The vial itself wobbled precariously just out of Tiger's reach.

With a horrendous sound of twisting metal, the weapon began to shudder violently. The noise rattled Tiger's skull, but he tried to ignore it and thrust the stun-stick against a second clamp. With an ear-splitting *bang*, the clamp broke in two, and he made a swipe for the vial, grabbing it before it dropped between the bars of the cage.

Tiger had no intention of hanging around. He climbed back down as the weapon above began to vibrate so erratically that metal panels fell from its side.

'It's going to blow!' screamed a technician as he lunged towards the subway door, where Aerialas and the other technician were already heading, and leapt inside for cover. The friends joined them just in time, sprinting down the spiral staircase. As the door to the subway sealed shut, the base of the super-weapon exploded in a magnificent ball of orange flame that blasted around the control room.

From the safety of the subway, everybody could feel the heat, but they were fortunately protected as the detonation continued to surge along the length of the cannon – destroying it in a colossal explosion that could be seen across the city.

Then silence.

Max was the first to clamber to his feet. Lights were flickering erratically and smoke was pouring down the stairs. 'Is everybody OK?'

He was answered by a series of groans as everybody slowly stood up, wiping the debris from themselves.

Tiger held up the thought vial. 'Got it!'

Before anybody could speak, Aerialas moved with startling speed. With a murderous cry, he grabbed the discarded stun-stick from the debris on the floor and struck Tiger in the shoulder. The jolt threw Tiger against the wall, where he crumpled, groaning in pain. Aerialas caught the vial before it hit the floor. He rounded on the surprised friends and waved the stun-stick threateningly.

'Try anything and I will fry you like your traitorous friend here,' snarled Aerialas as he fled towards the door at the other end of the corridor – but blocking the door was the huge form of Captain Crankshaft. 'Aerialas, at long last,' growled Crankshaft.

Aerialas raised the stun-stick – but Crankshaft's mechanical hand shot up and grabbed the middle of the weapon, bending it backwards so the crackling tip struck Aerialas's chest as he squeezed the trigger. With a grunt, Aerialas dropped to the floor, completely unconscious.

'I think he's shocked to see me,' said Crankshaft with a grin.

The pirates swiftly seized control of Eagle Mount and by dawn they had Aerialas bound in the main city square where the slowly massing crowds of bewildered citizens could see him.

Crankshaft announced they were all now free of the tyrant, and he declared there would be elections by the end of the week so the people could appoint a new, fair, leader. From the way everybody cheered, Max guessed that Crankshaft himself would be a strong candidate.

Once the celebrations were over, the friends met Crankshaft for a final farewell.

'You are one brave sky-lubber,' Crankshaft said, laying a hand on Tiger's shoulder.

Tiger winced: his shoulder and arms still hurt from the effects of the stun-stick. 'You think I'd make a good pirate?'

Crankshaft laughed. 'The best, matey.' Then he pointed to the thought vial wrapped in a cloth that Cat held. 'Make sure ye take that very far from 'ere. I don't wanna see the likes of it again.'

'We will,' said Cat, hugging Crankshaft.

Max shook hands with the captain then turned to his friends. 'Ready to go home?' They all nodded.

Home. The thought of home had never sounded

more appealing to the friends. All except Ant, who had enjoyed his time with the pirates so much that he secretly longed to stay a little while longer. He saluted Captain Crankshaft.

'Maybe I'll see you again,' said Ant.

'I hope so. I tell ye what, I don't think I'll be needing this again,' said Crankshaft, and placed his captain's hat on Ant's head. It was too large and fell over his eyes, but Ant managed to angle it so he could see. 'I think you'll make a grand captain,' Crankshaft added with a wink.

Ant took the hat off and examined it. Him, a captain? He smiled; there were a lot of universes out there … anything was possible.

NEXT … OUT OF THE FLAMES